Geology Rocks!

A Musical Play for Kids

Script, teacher's guide, and audio recording
with songs and instrumental accompaniment

Ron Fink and John Heath

Illustrations by Bert Davis

Bad Wolf Press
Camarillo, California

Special thanks to Brenda Tzipori who sang on songs 1, 4, 6, and 8, and Mike Fishell who played all instruments on songs 2, 3, and 5.

A Word About Copyright and Copying

From the Authors

We've spent a tremendous amount of time writing this musical, so we hope that you will do the honest thing and avoid illegal copying. Please encourage your friends and colleagues to purchase their very own copies rather than steal from friendly writers such as us.

Bad Wolf Press
5391 Spindrift Court
Camarillo, California 93012
Toll free: 1-888-827-8661
www.badwolfpress.com

ISBN 1-886588-27-9

BWP 0250

Table of Contents

Song List

Geology Rocks!

By Ron Fink and John Heath

The duration of the show is about 25 minutes

CHARACTERS:

Rosie
Jenn
Sherlock Holmes
Dr. Watson
Volcanoes
Earth
Ferns
Sea Shore
Canyon
Valley
Mountains
Snow White
Igneous Rock
Sedimentary Rock
Metamorphic Rock
Professor Rock

and a CHORUS comprised of all students who are not
playing roles on stage at the time

FLEXIBLE CASTING:
From 11-40 students.
Use as many Volcanoes, Ferns, etc. as
desired. One student can easily play
several roles if needed. Note that all
roles can be played by either boys or
girls; see our comments on page 35 of
the *Teacher's Guide*.

(STUDENTS walk quickly back and forth across stage, apparently searching for something or someone. Finally one STUDENT stops and loudly says:)

ROSIE: Let's face it—our geology teacher, Professor Rock, is missing!

CLASS (sings):

Song 1

Now we've searched high and we've searched low
So where on earth could that man go?
Our Professor Rock has disappeared.

We have not found a clue or trail
A zero on the Richter scale
Our Professor Rock has disappeared.

He loves he loves volcanoes
He loves he loves glaciers too
Earthquakes make him laugh
He hugs his seismograph
Every dinner that he ate
Was on a tectonic plate.

Now everywhere we turn we see
A geologic mystery

ONE STUDENT: Hey look I found some pieces of his beard!

STUDENTS (shout): How weird!

CLASS:

Is he a victim of basalt?
Or is it San Andreas' fault?
Our Professor Rock has disappeared.

He loves he loves volcanoes
He loves he loves glaciers too
Earthquakes make him laugh
He hugs his seismograph
Every dinner that he ate
Was on a tectonic plate.

Doo doo doo doo
Doo doo doo doo
Doo doo doo doo doo doo doo doo doo
Our Professor Rock has disappeared
Disa-
Disappeared.

(TWO STUDENTS remain on stage.)

ROSIE: What are we going to do, Jenn?

JENN: I don't know, Rosie. Professor Rock's disappearance is a complete mystery.

(SHERLOCK HOLMES and DR. WATSON enter. HOLMES is dressed like, well, Sherlock Holmes. Maybe he has a magnifying glass. Watson has a notebook and pen.)

HOLMES: A mystery you say? Then we've come to the right place.

ROSIE: Who are you?

WATSON: Excuse us. Holmes likes dramatic entrances.

JENN: Holmes? Sherlock Holmes?

HOLMES: Precisely! Dr. Watson and I have come to solve the mystery of your missing rock.

(HE picks up a rock and begins to examine it carefully with his magnifying glass.)

ROSIE: It's not a rock but a person, our teacher Professor Rock.

HOLMES: Silence! My astonishing powers of deduction have led me to a clue right here in this rock!

WATSON: What is it Holmes? Igneous? Metamorphic?

HOLMES: Sedimentary, my dear Watson.

    (MUSIC to "Geologic Time" begins here. The next lines are spoken over the music.)

JENN: Can you help us? We really need to find the Professor.

ROSIE: We've got to start searching right away.

HOLMES: Patience! These things take time. Rome wasn't built in a day.

HOLMES and WATSON:

Song 2

The earth's been here five billion years
It's seen a lot of change
What used to be an ocean floor
Is now a mountain range.

The desert lands have come and gone
The dinosaurs are hushed

HOLMES:

My brilliant brain needs time as well
My genius can't be rushed!

HOLMES and WATSON:

Geologic, geologic
Geologic time
Geologic, geologic
Geologic time

WATSON:
He's slow as rock

HOLMES and WATSON:

So set the clock
For geologic time.

The Colorado river runs
Ten million years it creeps
And bit by bit a canyon forms
That's over one mile deep.

The desert lands have come and gone
The dinosaurs are hushed

HOLMES:

My brilliant brain needs time as well
My genius can't be rushed!

HOLMES, WATSON, and CHORUS:

Geologic, geologic
Geologic time
Geologic, geologic
Geologic time

WATSON:
He's slow as rock

HOLMES, WATSON, and CHORUS:

So set the clock
For geologic time.

WATSON:
He's slow as rock

HOLMES, WATSON, and CHORUS:

So set the clock
For geologic time.

HOLMES: Come along, Watson. We must find that rock. We'll start by interviewing some pebbles I spotted in the driveway—they looked suspicious.

WATSON: Splendid, Holmes.
          (writing in his notebook as THEY exit)
I shall call this, The Case of the Runaway Rock.
          (THEY exit)

JENN: Rosie, I don't think they're going to be much help.

ROSIE: No. We'll have to find Professor Rock on our own.

JENN: Right. Professor Rock has been working near some volcanoes—maybe we should talk to them.

ROSIE: Great idea.

          (THEY walk around until they meet the VOLCANOES, who have entered.)

JENN: There they are!

ROSIE: Hello, volcanoes. Have you seen Professor Rock?

VOLCANO #1: He was here just a few days ago, checking up on us. We haven't been feeling well.

ROSIE: I can see. You don't look so hot.

VOLCANO #2: Oh no, we're TOO hot. That's the problem.

VOLCANOES:

I ain't well
Can't you tell?
I'm belching steam and ashes
With molten molten molten rock
Molten rock and gases.

Song 3

I ain't well
See me swell?
I think it's something drastic
I'm feeling feeling feeling aaach!
Feeling pyroclastic.

Magma coming up my vent
Lava pouring out
Here it comes
I need a Tums ™
Before I blow my spout.

I ain't well
Can't you help?
I'm crackin' and I'm swellin'
I feel like feel like feel like whoa!
Feel like Mt. St. Helens.

(VOLCANOES do dance during instrumental)

Did we say "dance"? Yes we did, but we didn't necessarily mean it. Please see our comments on page 40 of the *Teacher's Guide*.

Magma coming up my vent
Lava pouring out
Here it comes
I need a Tums
Before I blow my spout.

VOLCANOES and CHORUS:

I ain't well
Can't you tell?
I'm belching steam and ashes
With molten molten molten rock
Molten rock and gases.
With molten molten molten rock
Molten rock and gases.

(VOLCANOES exit)

ROSIE: Wow. That must be some fever if it's hot enough to melt rock.

EARTH (from side of stage): That's nothin', baby. I'm 12,000 degrees down in my core.

JENN: Who said that?

EARTH (entering): I did, honey. I'm the Earth.

JENN: The earth?

ROSIE: But how'd you get so hot? I thought you were just continents and water.

EARTH: Isn't that typical?! I've got 4000 miles down to my core, and all you folks ever think about is my outer 40 miles.

ROSIE: I'm sorry.

EARTH: Below my crust I've got a mantel, an outer core AND an inner core. You've got to look below the surface.

I am deep
Not just water and some dust   (Song 4)
I am deep
I've got spunk beneath my crust.

I am deep
Though my surface may seem mild
I am deep
You should see my inner child!

My mantle is so hot and wild, rocks just melt and ooze
At my core you'll find a gal who loves to sing the blues.

I am deep
Miles and miles of hidden space
I am not
Just another pretty face.

CHORUS:

She's deep
She is deep
She's deep
She is deep
She's deep
She is deep.
She's deep
She is deep.

EARTH and CHORUS:

Yes I'm deep
Not just water and some dust
I am deep
I've got spunk beneath my crust.

JENN: You haven't seen Professor Rock, have you?

EARTH: You mean some funny little dude with a beard who talks to volcanoes?

ROSIE: Yes!

EARTH: I saw him just yesterday with some Ferns. I don't trust Ferns—there's something shady about them.
(Exits)

JENN: Thanks!

ROSIE: Come on, let's go talk to those Ferns.

(THEY start to move across stage, but are interrupted by the appearance of HOLMES and WATSON)

HOLMES: I think we're onto something, Watson.

WATSON: Excellent tracking, Holmes

HOLMES (shouts out): Stop! Don't move!

WATSON (freezes): What is it? A clue?

HOLMES (uncomfortable): No. I've got some sand in my shorts and it's killing me.

JENN: Mr. Holmes! Have you found anything yet?

HOLMES: I'm afraid your rock has eluded us so far. But we HAVE found some gravel, an old tire, and a toaster oven. Care for some garlic bread?

ROSIE: No, you still don't understand. We're looking for PROFESSOR Rock—he's our geology...

HOLMES (interrupting): Come along, Watson. We can't stand around here all day eating garlic bread. There's a rock to find!
	(THEY converse as they exit)

WATSON: Excellent!
	(writing in his notebook)
I think I shall call this The Case of the Missing Marble.

HOLMES: Are you sure it's marble? Could be limestone, old boy. Or granite.

WATSON (as THEY disappear): I once knew a granite in India. Rather odd chap, really. Wanted to become a sink.
	(THEY exit.)

ROSIE (to JENN): Come on, Jenn, let's go talk to those Ferns.

	(THEY walk around stage until THEY run into the FERNS)

JENN: There they are. Hi. We were hoping you'd seen Professor Rock.

FERN #1 (ALL FERNS act guilty): Who? Professor Rock? I don't know any Professor Rock, do you?

FERN #2: Who me? No, uh-uh, no way. Never heard of him.

FERN #3: Me neither. I'm just a fern.

ALL THREE FERNS (mumbling quickly, loudly, separately and over each other, sounding very dumb): Yep, just a fern, just a fern, fern, fern, fern.

ROSIE: Hey, look over here.
        (SHE stoops over and picks up a pair of glasses)
These look just like Professor Rock's glasses.

JENN: Yeah, they do.
        (to FERNS)
Are you sure you haven't seen Professor Rock?

FERN #1: What, those glasses? They belong to, uh, me. Yeah. That's right. They're mine.

ROSIE: Since when do Ferns need glasses?

FERN #2: Uh, well, see, we've got lots of time on our hands. So we, uh, read the newspaper.

JENN: Ferns read the newspaper?

FERN #3: Yeah, we're especially interested in the energy crisis.

FERN #1: We've got a plan for solving it: we're gonna become fossil fuel!

ROSIE: What?

FERN #3: That's right. See, we're just waiting here to decompose, sink down into the earth, and turn into fossil fuel. It's gonna happen, y'know.

FERN #1: Just think of it. Eventually we'll become natural gas, oil, and coal. I can't wait.

FERNS:

Song 5

Oh to be a fossil fuel
You know that would be cool
You just have to lie there
Set down roots and die there
You don't even have to go to school
Oh, oh, oh, oh to be a fossil fuel.
Yeah, yeah, yeah, yeah to be a fossil fuel.

Oh to be a fossil fuel
You know that would be cool
Heating homes in winter
Cooking up your dinner
Is that brocc'li? Man your mom is cruel!
Oh, oh, oh, oh to be a fossil fuel.
Yeah, yeah, yeah, yeah to be a fossil fuel.

I just want to be
In your SUV
Everyone can see…you're gonna need a lot of me!

(FERNS do FERN dance
during instrumental)

FERNS and CHORUS:

Oh to be a fossil fuel
You know that would be cool
They are disappearing
So we're volunteering
In a million years we'll heat your pool
Oh, oh, oh, oh to be a fossil fuel.
Yeah, yeah, yeah, yeah to be a fossil fuel.

JENN: Are you sure you haven't seen Professor Rock?

FERN #3: Why don't you check out those little miners up in the mountains?

FERN #1: Yeah! Those little guys are very strange.

FERN #2: If Professor Rock…

ALL THREE (look at audience): …Whoever THAT is…

FERN #2: …ran into those guys while they were digging up precious metals and ores, he could be in big trouble.

ROSIE: Where do these miners live?

FERN #3: Way up there, in the mountains.

(FERNS exit)

JENN: I guess we'd better check it out.

(THEY start to head across stage)

ROSIE: Those Ferns were acting pretty weird. Hey, who's this?

(VALLEY, SEA SHORE, and CANYON enter)

SEA SHORE: Hello. I'm the Sea Shore.

CANYON: I'm a Canyon.

VALLEY (peppy): And I'm Valley girl. It's like totally awesome to meet you.

JENN: We're trying to find our professor. He's missing.

SEA SHORE: Maybe he eroded.

ROSIE: Eroded?

CANYON: Sure. That's what happened to us. Although it usually takes a long time for sand or water to wear someone down completely.

VALLEY: Like for SURE! I mean, hellOOO! I was like sitting there for SO long—BORING—then this MEGA-huge glacier came and now I'm like a total babe. We LOVE erosion.

VALLEY, SEA SHORE, and CANYON:

Song 6

Wind
Rain
Ice
Waves
Erosion has carved out this land

Wind
Rain
Ice
Waves
Erosion
Erosion
Erosion makes me what I am.

Wind
Rain
Ice
Waves
Erosion has carved out this land

Wind
Rain
Ice
Waves
Erosion
Erosion
Erosion makes me what I am.

SEA SHORE:
Without the ocean pounding me I wouldn't curve like so
        (SEA SHORE bends)

CANYON: Without a river sculpting me I'd still be a plateau.

VALLEY:
Without a glacier gouging me I'd be a hilly spot

ALL THREE:
We owe ev'rything we are to ev'rything that we are not!

17

ALL THREE and CHORUS:

Wind
Rain
Ice
Waves
Erosion has carved out this land.

Wind
Rain
Ice
Waves
Erosion
Erosion
Erosion makes me what I am.
Erosion makes me what I am.

      (Exit. MOUNTAIN #1 enters.)

JENN: Come on, there's the mountain.

ROSIE: It's awfully big.

      (HOLMES and WATSON enter)

HOLMES: The search is over! I have found your missing rock!

WATSON: Brilliant, Holmes.
      (pause, looks around)
Where?

HOLMES: Right in front of your face, my good doctor.
      (points to MOUNTAIN)

MOUNTAIN #1: Me? Well, technically, I'm a mountain.

HOLMES: Exactly. Permit me to demonstrate my powers of
deduction.

WATSON: Excellent. Wait! Let me get this down.
      (pulls out notebook)

HOLMES: Are you, or are you not, a mountain?

MOUNTAIN #2: I thought we just did that.

HOLMES: But you're far more than just a mountain, aren't you? From the way you pronounce your vowels I can tell you are left-handed. But you did not shake hands with me with your left hand. From this I deduce that you have a cousin named Matilda who is allergic to chickweed. And chickweed, as Dr. Watson can tell you, is used only by the TeeTee tribe in northwest Guinea to reduce the level of stress in ducks. And THIS can ONLY mean that you are NOT just a mountain, BUT A ROCK!

MOUNTAIN #1: Well, yes, I AM made of rock.

HOLMES: Ah ha! Just as I thought! Come on, Watson, we're finished here.

JENN: Hey wait!

HOLMES: No need to thank us. We told you we'd find your rock, and find your rock we did.

(MOUNTAIN #2 enters and stands next to #1)

WATSON: I think I shall call this The Case of the Mutinous Mountain.

(as THEY exit)

HOLMES: It WAS a rather large rock, wasn't it Watson?

WATSON: Enormous.

HOLMES: Can't imagine how they didn't spot it. You never can tell with Yanks, can you?
(THEY exit)

ROSIE: Maybe now we can finally find the Professor.

JENN: Wait a minute! Where'd that other mountain come from?

MOUNTAIN #2: Hi there. I've been growing here for quite a while.

ROSIE: Mountains GROW?

MOUNTAIN #1: Sure. Holmes was right about that— we ARE made of rock. The earth's crust is made up of lots of gigantic plates that sort of float and move on the mantel.

MOUNTAIN #2: These plates carry the continents on their backs—so they're called continental plates.

MOUNTAIN #1: And when two continental plates bump into each other, the squish together and make folded mountains, like us.

MOUNTAIN #2: And earthquake faults form where the two plates come together. It's so exciting—the earth is moving all the time!

MOUNTAINS:

Some continental plates collide
And though it may be slow
They crunch and fold and soon enough
The Himalayas grow.

Song 7

Sometimes the plates will slide and shake
Like they do in L.A.
A few more quakes, that town will be
In San Francisco Bay.

Love them plates
Oh love them plates
These continental sledges
They're rumblin' rumblin' rumblin' at
Rumblin' at the edges.

Love them plates
Oh love them plates
These continental sledges
They're rumblin' rumblin' rumblin' at
Rumblin' at the edges.

Some continental plates collide
And though it may be slow
They crunch and fold and soon enough
The Himalayas grow.

The continents are on the go
They creep and jump and slide
So pick a continental plate
And take it for a ride.

MOUNTAINS and CHORUS:

Love them plates
Oh love them plates
These continental sledges
They're rumblin' rumblin' rumblin' at
Rumblin' at the edges.

Love them plates
Oh love them plates
These continental sledges
They're rumblin' rumblin' rumblin' at
Rumblin' at the edges.

(MOUNTAINS exit)

JENN (to ROSIE): Come on, now that we're in the mountains we've got to find those miners.

ROSIE (pointing ahead): Who is that?

SNOW WHITE: Hello.

JENN: Hi. Have you seen any miners around here?

SNOW WHITE: Not recently, I'm afraid.

ROSIE: So they used to be here?

SNOW WHITE: Oh my yes, a long time ago. Seven of the cutest little dwarves you've ever seen.

JENN: Dwarves? Uh, who are you?

SNOW WHITE: I'm Snow White.

ROSIE: Snow White? You mean, THE Snow White? The one with the wicked step-mother and the apple?

SNOW WHITE: And the seven dwarves.

JENN: I remember them. They had these funny little names. What were they? Slappy? Cheezy?

ROSIE: Yeah, that's right. There was Frumpy, and Icky, and…

SNOW WHITE: Oh no. You're thinking of their stage names.

JENN: Stage names?

SNOW WHITE: When they got a role in a movie, the studio changed their names. Good PR. But their real name was Herbert.

ROSIE: All of them?

SNOW WHITE: Yes. Although most of them liked to be called Herb.

JENN: That must have been confusing.

SNOW WHITE: But it was so easy to remember. And they all looked alike. The only thing different about them was they all dug for different kinds of minerals and ores.

ROSIE: So they're not here?

SNOW WHITE: No. All my little Herbs gave up mining long ago.

One Herb got an allergy
And sold his silver mine
One gave up on iron-ore
And now sells shoes on-line.

One of them could not find coal
One got tooth decay
One Herb bagged his search for gold
Became a CPA.

Seven little miners
With something new to try
Seven little miners
Good-bye.

One Herb lost his diamond mine
And never was the same
Number seven slips my mind
But Herbert was his name.

As for me I used to clean
While they went out to dig
Then I met a handsome prince
And got a better gig.

Seven little miners
With something new to try
Seven little miners
Good-bye.

#1 HALF-CHORUS: Copper, aluminum, nickel, lead
#2 HALF-CHORUS: Opal, sapphire, emerald, ruby
#1 HALF-CHORUS: Copper, aluminum, nickel, lead
#2 HALF-CHORUS: Opal, sapphire, emerald, ruby
#1 HALF-CHORUS: Copper, aluminum, nickel, lead
#2 HALF-CHORUS: Opal, sapphire, emerald, ruby

SNOW WHITE and CHORUS:

Seven little miners
With something new to try
Seven little miners
Good-bye.
Seven little miners
Good-bye.

    (SNOW WHITE exits)

JENN: What now? Professor Rock isn't here.

ROSIE: I want to talk to the Ferns again. I didn't believe a word they said.

JENN: You think they did something to Professor Rock? I hope they didn't hurt him.

ROSIE: We've got to get back there fast.

JENN: But it's a long way back down the mountain.

    (ROCKS enter)

IGNEOUS: Excuse me, but perhaps we can help.

ROSIE (looking over the ROCKS): Thanks, but I don't think so.

SEDIMENTARY: Why not?

ROSIE: Well, mostly because you're ROCKS.

METAMORPHIC: So?

ROSIE: So?! We need to find some way to get down this mountain as fast as possible to save our Professor. And you rocks just kind of sit there all day.

IGNEOUS: Outrageous!

SEDIMENTARY: Preposterous!

METAMORPHIC: Why I never!

IGNEOUS: You've clearly never heard of the rock cycle.

JENN: The rock cycle?

SEDIMENTARY: We rocks are always changing.

METAMORPHIC (still upset): Why I never!

ROSIE: I didn't mean to insult you.

IGNEOUS: Molten rock cools and becomes Igneous rock. Like me. Then erosion and weathering chip away small pieces that settle at the bottom of bodies of water.

SEDIMENTARY: That's where I come in. These pieces form layers of sediment. They get compressed and squeezed, and eventually—voila—you've got me, Sedimentary rock, like limestone.

METAMORPHIC (still upset): Why I never!

ROSIE: Sorry! Look, we're in a hurry!

METAMORPHIC: I'll sum up quickly. Eventually my friend Sedimentary gets buried deep in the earth. With some heat and pressure he gets harder and heavier, and then I emerge, Metamorphic rock. Marble is limestone that's become metamorphic.

IGNEOUS: And finally metamorphic rock gets heated and mixed in the earth and comes back as yours truly once again. It's a cycle. Get it?

JENN: Well, that's interesting. But how can you help us get down the mountain?

SEDIMENTARY: Haven't you been listening? We're always on the move. Just hop on the rock cycle!

ROCKS:

Folks say rocks are dull as dirt
Say we're slow oh man that hurts
Say we're boring and inert
As a lump of coal

Folks should take a longer view
Watch a million years or two
All the changes we go through
We can rock and roll!

CHORUS: Rock rock rock cycle

ROCKS: Cycling through the years

CHORUS: Rock rock rock cycle

ROCKS: Cycling without gears

CHORUS: Rock rock rock cycle

ROCKS: Through the earth we are spread

CHORUS: Rock rock rock cycle

ROCKS: Who says rock is dead?

ROCKS and CHORUS:

Folks say rocks are dull as dirt
Say we're slow oh man that hurts
Say we're boring and inert
As a lump of coal

Folks should take a longer view
Watch a million years or two
All the changes we go through
We can rock and roll!

CHORUS: Rock rock rock cycle

ROCKS: Cycling through the years

CHORUS: Rock rock rock cycle

ROCKS: Cycling without gears

CHORUS: Rock rock rock cycle

ROCKS: Through the earth we are spread

CHORUS: Rock rock rock cycle

ROCKS and CHORUS: Who says rock is dead?

During this chorus, ROSIE and JENN follow the ROCKS across stage, as if being lead down the mountain by them.

(ROCKS exit. The GIRLS wave good-bye.)

JENN (to the ROCKS): Thank you for the ride.

(FERNS enter)

ROSIE: Now where are those ferns?

JENN: There they are! What have you done with Professor Rock?

FERN #1: Professor Rock? Who's Professor Rock?

ROSIE: Don't play innocent with us. Where is he?

FERN #2: We don't know any Professor Rock.

(PROFESSOR ROCK stumbles onto the stage, the GIRLS spot him)

ROSIE and JENN: Professor Rock!

FERNS: Oh, THAT Professor Rock.

JENN: Professor, are you okay? What happened?

PROFESSOR ROCK: Jenn, Rosie. It's so good to see you. I was doing research over here on geo-thermal energy and these ferns kidnapped me.

ROSIE: Why?

PROFESSOR ROCK: Geo-thermal energy comes from tapping into the hot water and steam inside the earth. It's clean, renewable, and efficient. The Ferns were afraid that people would stop using fossil fuels if alternatives were used.

FERN: Ha! You don't believe THAT? Well, do you?

(ROSIE, JENN, and PROFESSOR ROCK all look at FERNS disapprovingly)

FERNS (sing first line of their song, without musical accompaniment): Oh to be a fossil fuel, you know that would be cool…

JENN (to FERNS): You've been very bad ferns.
(shaking finger at FERNS, as if THEY were misbehaving dogs)
Bad ferns.

(FERNS look sheepish)

ROSIE: Don't you have something to say to the Professor?

FERNS (pause, then heads down, kicking ground): We're sorry for kidnapping you, Professor Rock.

JENN: That's better. Oh Professor Rock, I'm so glad you're okay.

ROSIE: And we learned so much about geology today.

PROFESSOR ROCK: I can't wait to hug my seismograph!

PROFESSOR ROCK:

I thank you all for finding me
A geologic mystery

CLASS:

Our Professor Rock has re-appeared.

PROFESSOR ROCK:

You'd think by now I would have learned
You just can't turn your back on ferns

CLASS:

Our Professor Rock has re-appeared.

He loves he loves volcanoes
He loves he loves glaciers too
Earthquakes make him laugh
He hugs his seismograph

ONE STUDENT (rapping):

Every dinner that he ate
Was on a tectonic plate.
One two three four.

CLASS:

We learned a lot about the earth
There's so much more than sea and dirt

ANOTHER STUDENT (holding up socks): I kept Sherlock's socks
as souvenirs!

CLASS (shout): How weird!

CLASS:

Yeah we searched low and we searched high
We found our geo-thermal guy
Our Professor Rock has re-appeared.

He loves he loves volcanoes
He loves he loves glaciers too
Earthquakes make him laugh
He hugs his seismograph

ONE STUDENT (rapping):

Every dinner that he ate
Was on a tectonic plate.
One two three four.

CLASS:

Doo doo doo doo
Doo doo doo doo
Doo doo doo doo doo doo doo doo
Our Professor Rock has re-appeared
Re-a-
Re-appeared.

The End

Teacher's Guide

Introduction

Geology Rocks! is a musical/opera designed to be performed by elementary school classes, particularly by students in second through sixth grade. The older students will of course do a more polished job, but please don't be afraid of having your younger students perform this show. They'll have a great time (this is not your regular school play) and their parents will have a ball.

In fact, one of the really nice things about this musical play is the response you'll get from parents. You'll find them grateful for the opportunity to see their child perform in a truly fun show full of melody and wit. Indeed, rumor has it that some parents have so thoroughly enjoyed the performance that they have had to have the smiles surgically removed from their faces in order to be taken seriously at work.

If you're an experienced producer of classroom shows, then *Geology Rocks!* will be a snap. If you're new to this sort of thing, relax! Putting on a play is a wonderful experience for your kids, and it's a heck of a lot easier than you probably think. This introduction is designed to provide you with all the necessary tips for a smooth and joyous production. We consulted teachers whose classes have performed our shows and asked them what they wished they had known before they started. We listened carefully, and now it's all here for you.

Even if you can't sing or play an instrument! Honest! We know a teacher who has successfully produced a number of musicals in her classes without singing or playing a note (she's very shy). All you have to do is move your lips! Remember, the audio recording demonstrates all the songs.

Doing a little script-tease

We strongly suggest that you do not send home copies of the script with each student. The problem is that the parents will read the script and when they come to watch the play, well, they'll already know what to expect. We think your best bet is to copy only the lyrics and narrations for your actors. Let Mom and Dad help their child learn their parts, but give your parents the gift of being pleasantly surprised when they see the performance.

Getting Started

Figure on about a month from first introduction to final performance. This may sound like a lot of time, but remember that most of the days you won't work for very long, perhaps just singing a few songs together. We have an example of one reasonable Timetable on page 37. We suggest that you play the recording of the show for several days before you start singing songs. Then after the kids get the hang of the songs, you can sing them whenever the class has a few extra

minutes. When you get around to casting and staging the show you'll need more time again. You'll also want to schedule additional time for the creation of sets, props, and costumes (if you decide to use them—see our advice below).

Lately educators have been talking about teaching "across the curriculum," that is, using large projects and themes to connect the various skills and subjects to be studied. *Geology Rocks!* is ideal for this since you can easily connect art, music, earth science, and even reading under the guise of a fun show.

Is *Friendly Neighborhood Helpers* an opera or a musical?

And what's the difference, anyway? According to our dictionary, in an opera most or all of the story is sung, but in a musical the dialogue plays the more important role. Beyond that, musicals tend to be written in a popular style while operas are supposed to be "artistic." In truth, there's no meaningful distinction and you can call this show whatever you like without offending us. (The composer refers to it as an opera, while the lyricist insists it is a musical. Go figure.)

Now, relax and have some fun. We've written this show so you can get out of it what you want. If you choose to work very hard, managing every detail—go ahead! Really! You'll probably have a high quality performance. But make sure that's the level of activity and stress you're comfortable with. Don't let the parents turn this into a Broadway production. You can also choose to be low-key about it all. Tell yourself that these are just kids, your audience isn't paying fifty dollars a ticket, and you won't have a perfect show. You'll stay more relaxed and enjoy the experience. It just depends upon your own personality and the students themselves. No matter how you approach *Geology Rocks!*, remember it's the process which is important for the students' education: the reading, creating, singing, thinking, and developing self-esteem that go into learning the show are the real point to the final performance anyway. There's no reason you shouldn't have as much fun doing all this as your students!

Here's a bit of time-tested advice if you're new to this type of musical production: get another teacher at your school to put on *Geology Rocks!* at the same time. You can share sets and costumes and bounce ideas off one another. Your classes can watch each other rehearse and the students can give feedback to their peers. This process has proven to be a great aid to novice directors, and students learn a lot by participating in the assessment and development of the show (more on this later).

Some teachers like to have as much parental help in the classroom as possible; others prefer to work with the kids without interference. Wherever you fall on this continuum, you'll probably find it useful to ask for a certain amount of help. Be sure you send a parents' letter at the onset of the project. Include performance dates and tell exactly what sort of assistance you'll be looking for. If putting on plays is new to your school, you may want to outline some of the educational advantages as well.

Music (and the enclosed CD)

The audio recording is a teaching tool for helping your children learn all the songs. The first recorded version features the composer and a talented friend brilliantly singing the songs with dazzling musical accompaniment. The second version of the show has just the accompaniments to all the songs (played stunningly by the composer and another talented friend, both of whom were blindfolded and drinking a glass of water during the entire recording. Amazing, aren't they?).

We suggest you introduce the music to your class by playing the recording during a class work session. You might do this several times, starting well in advance of your actual rehearsal of the show. The music will seem easy and familiar when your students finally begin to sing the songs. Have *all* your students learn *all* the songs. This is much more fun for the class, and it will give you great flexibility in casting and substituting for absent performers.

Ready for some controversy? The easiest way of getting older students to learn the show is probably to copy the script and give it to them. Some teachers, however, like to write all the lyrics to the songs on large poster-size sheets. This is a lot of work. If you choose to do this, we have two suggestions: get some parents to divide the work between them, or photocopy the lyrics onto transparencies and use an overhead projector. Other teachers like the students to learn the songs by ear without looking at the script.. Play the songs for a week or so during class, and then play the version of the recording without the words. You'll be surprised how well students respond to the challenge of singing along.

Using a musician

If you know of a parent or other community member who might be willing to play piano or guitar, contact them early. Play them the CD and show them the samples of music on page 45 of this book to be certain they are comfortable with it (to order the sheet music for *Geology Rocks!*, use the enclosed order form). Another option is to hire a professional. You may find someone to work for less than you'd think — even starving musicians like to help the schools. Maybe you can get some money from your school PTA. Regardless of who your musician is, paid or not, be sure to schedule at least one rehearsal with them before the performance. Your students will need to get used to the sound of a live player, and the musician needs to learn the cues and get a sense of what the children sound like.

You can perform the show to great applause by simply using the accompanying recording. If you choose to use the CD for the performance, get a volunteer to be in charge of boombox. It's very important that this be the same person throughout the rehearsals and the final performance. The volunteer needs a script and lots of practice with the class. If you can't find a parent, then try to snag an older student. Don't try to handle this yourself—you need to keep your eyes on the students and be free to solve problems as they occur.

If you have access to the right equipment you can manufacture copies of the entire recording. Please don't! It's strictly illegal, absolutely immoral, and government tests indicate it is probably fattening. Really, we expect better things from someone as nice as you. (Did you see our Official Policy on fair use, photocopying and audio duplication on the second page? It's a masterful blend of tact, threat, and blatant begging, so maybe this would be a good time to review it.) What you *can* do is copy *one or two songs* for any student. Better still, record the song five times in a row on the student's tape (ask them to bring one from home) and have him or her sing along with the tape daily. This kind of repetition really helps. Songs sung by soloists and groups can be copied and studied in the same way.

Casting

Geology Rocks! was originally written to be performed by a class of from eighteen to thirty kids, but the show is very flexible. How many Volcanoes are there? How many Ferns? Three? Five? (One teacher we know insists that odd numbers work best, and who are we to argue?) Experiment a bit, keeping at least one strong singer in each group. We recommend that you don't create groups with more than seven students, or the stage begins to look and sound like a rugby scrum.

We suggest waiting until the last week or two before you pick specific children for each part. We don't recommend a formal audition. Instead, let various children experiment with different roles and try out different combinations. Perhaps a few friends will discover they enjoy singing "Erosion" together. Or perhaps several children will express interest in the Rock Cycle. Our one recommendation is that if you choose to have soloists, be sure to pick actors who can sing loudly enough to be heard over a possibly noisy audience.

As you know, some children are a little shy about performing and especially about singing in public. (The lyricist intentionally swallowed his history book in the third grade in order to be excused from singing "I've Got A Hammer" in front of the class.) You might want to ask if there are any children who would prefer a speaking part instead of a singing one. Respect their fears, but if you provide regular opportunities for performance you'll be pleased to see your students gain confidence.

Eventually, of course, you'll need to make a choice and probably a student or two will feel hurt by the selection. We have attempted to write in as many parts as possible and to spread the singing roles evenly throughout the cast, but somebody is still bound to be disappointed. Try to help them understand that the selection in no way reflects poorly on them. If you put on more than one performance each year you will be able to give different children the opportunity to have a "starring" role.

Blending Genders

Do not feel bound by gender in your casting of these or any parts. All the parts in this show — with the possible exception of Snow White — can be played by boys or girls or any combination. You might need to change a few pronouns here and there. And don't hesitate to add actors or double up roles if that works best for the size of your class.

Costumes

You don't really *need* any costumes, but most kids (and certainly most audiences) like them. However there is a very real danger that some parents will start competing with each other to provide the fanciest costumes. We suggest that when you first tell parents about the play, explain that the costumes will be designed by you and the class, and so please don't send in any costume without asking you first. Try to be firm on this.

The fancier the costumes, the more self-conscious the performers and the quieter they will sing. (As you may have guessed by now, getting some of your students to project their voices to the audience will be one of your challenges.) Make sure what they wear is comfortable, especially the hats (which, unless they fit perfectly, tend to be very distracting). Keep hats—and wigs—to a minimum. In general, beards are a bad idea. When in doubt, simplify. (We think decorated t-shirts and baseball caps can cover just about any costuming needs. Of course, we are biased—our own wardrobe still consists mostly of t-shirts and baseball caps.)

For *Geology Rocks!*,the simplest thing for most of the characters (i.e. the geologic features)—indeed, our strong recommendation—would be to hang a cardboard plaque around the actors' necks that said "Volcano" or "Sea Shore" etc.. Kids dressed in giant cardboard cones are cute, we admit, but it's a dramatic disaster when they can't move around or feel so uncomfortable that they don't sing. Here are some ideas for the other characters:

JENN and ROSIE: They're students, so they really don't need any costumes.

SHERLOCK HOLMES and DR. WATSON: Actors can dress like these characters as seen in films and TV shows. Holmes has a distinctive hat, could wear a cape, and carry a magnifying glass. Watson is dressed quite properly, British style, and needs a notebook and pen.

PROFESSOR ROCK: A good hiking hat and boots, and some khaki pants and shirt. We've given him a beard and glasses, but this is optional. Beards can be a nuisance, so make it a very small one (or painted on).

SNOW WHITE: She's a former fairy-tale princess! Maybe a long skirt.

All actors playing geologic features should simply have signs hanging around their necks.

A Four-Week Timetable

Week One

1. 20 minutes a day listening to songs

Week Two

1. 20 minutes a day listening to and singing the songs
2. Review curriculum connections with class.
3. Maybe move to the songs a bit

Week Three

1. 30 minutes a day singing songs, moving around
2. Read script together, taking turns with different parts.
3. Plan physical production: costumes (if using), props, staging.
4. Half-way through the week ask students to write down or tell you the parts they most want (in order) and make your selections by the end of the week.

Week Four

1. One hour daily
2. Get the play on its feet where you will be performing.
3. Use masking tape to mark where students will be (you can color code).
4. Perform for another class and invite that class to write reviews.
5. Video the rehearsal/performances so your students can see and hear what they're really doing.
6. Do more performances for other classes. Aim for at least three performances in front of kids before performing for families.
7. Perform for families. Don't worry, it doesn't have to be perfect.
8. Don't worry, it doesn't have to be perfect.
9. Don't worry, it doesn't have to be perfect.

The Set

You don't really need a set to put on a successful performance, so don't worry. Here's one idea for set and staging in the classroom that has worked very well. (If you have access to an auditorium or stage, you will have a bit more flexibility.) If you want to make a "stage" so the audience can see better, you can put students' tables together.

Geology Rocks! does not have a "realistic" setting. That is, the action takes place in the mysterious place of theatrical convention. The show begins in what might be a classroom or office of Professor Rock. The action quickly moves outside, however, as we meet various geologic features. To indicate a change of scene you can simply have Jenn and Rosie walk back and forth a bit until they meet the next characters on their journey. No matter how you set it up, remember that all songs must be sung to the audience with the actors in the front, middle part of the stage. See our sample stage set-up on page 40. A banner across the back of the stage could read "Geology Rocks!"—this will let the audience know what's in store.

By all means have the kids do most of the set-planning and building—it's a great art project. If you can get some grown-up assistance the whole thing will flow smoothly and your kids will have a wonderful time. Once everything is ready they'll feel a real sense of pride and ownership.

Staging

If you have access to a real stage, then you can simply have the actors who are not performing wait off stage until it is time for them to enter. If you are performing in a classroom, however, with a large group and in a constricted space, you will probably have to keep all the actors on the "stage" at all times. You can have the students sit down until it is their turn to perform.

On the page 40 there is an aerial view of this kind of set-up in a classroom. You'll notice that the kids' chairs are being used by the audience (which is also probably sitting in front of the chairs as well as standing in back).

We've also positioned the students in groups on the stage. This is just one possibility. You'll need to experiment with this. The challenge is to place the students so they are not in the way when they are not performing, so they can get where they need to be easily during the show, so they can move about during their "numbers" as they need to, and so they can be heard when they sing. Here are a few ideas we've gathered from teachers who have performed our shows:

> ## The Joys of Masking Tape
>
> You will want to mark the spots on the stage where students are to stand and/or sit throughout the performance. These "marks" can easily be set out with masking tape on the floor. Mark where soloists, small groups, and the chorus will stand during each scene. This will keep everyone in place and make your job of managing thirty energetic actors

❖ Most of the action of the play—the singing, narration, and movement—should take place at the front of the stage. The audience cannot see or hear clearly what's going on in the back.

❖ Make certain that when the students sing they are facing the audience. They can move around, look at each other, do whatever you want before and after their song, but they must move to the front of the stage and face the audience when it is their turn to sing. They can stand side by side, or the taller ones can be behind the shorter ones, or those in front can sit down–whatever you like–but their mouths should be turned towards the front.

❖ Don't put all the actors and groups of actors in straight lines. This is not very exciting and too regimented—the stage begins to look like a face off between the British and the colonists in the Revolutionary War. Bunch them together in different formations as they wait for their moment to "star" at the front of the stage.

❖ Don't have the students "dance" while they are singing. Making music of any kind while moving is extremely difficult for anyone of any age to do. Moreover, the students are likely to turn away from the audience during their dance, and that, you will remember, is a no-no.

❖ And you'll notice we keep writing "dance" instead of dance. Isn't that annoying? The point here is that you don't have to choreograph a Broadway number and the students don't have to know anything about formal dance. We want you to think of this as an opportunity for MOVEMENT. What we're after, and the audience is craving, is some visual excitement to match the musical fun. No need to get fancy. When in doubt, think silly and simple.

Painted Backdrop

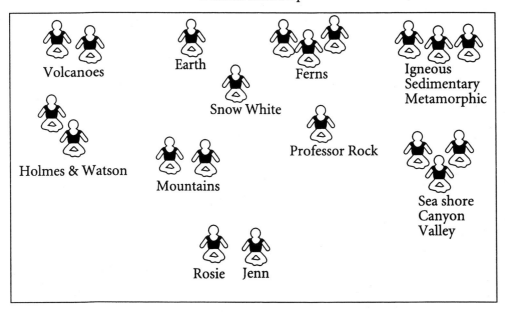

Teacher

Audience

40

Rehearsals and Assessment

After the students have learned the songs and the show has been cast, you will need to start teaching them where to stand and how and when to move. You will also need to work on individual songs, and especially on their behavior when they are NOT on center stage. Don't worry about the quality of the overall performance when you begin. Remember, this is all part of the learning process, so take advantage of the opportunities for teaching and assessment. Again, teachers have come up with a wonderful variety of ways to make rehearsals a central part of their students' learning. Here are some of their tips:

❖ Don't panic. Rehearsals early on, and even up to the day of the performance, can be quite rough. The kids will pull through when it counts.

❖ Each day ask the students to give suggestions on improvement: What can everyone do to make the show better?

❖ Ask the students to self-evaluate as well: How did I do my job? How can I do better next time? (This can be done verbally or in writing.)

❖ It is best to have several full dress rehearsals so students can get used to them. Do these in front of an audience so students learn to project.

❖ Videotape a rehearsal and have the students analyze it. What was good? What could have been done better? This is a very valuable tool. When the students see themselves fidgeting and fooling around, when they can't hear themselves sing, they will discover for themselves what they need to work on.

❖ Ask a student audience to think like a director and then write anonymous comments. It's surprising how helpful these comments can be.

> ## Third-Grade Kids Recommend the Following:
> * Everyone has to work together as a team.
> * Cast members don't need to give directions to others while on stage. It's distracting. Let the person have some "wait" time and the teacher will help get them back on track.
> * Don't worry about making a mistake. The audience probably won't pick it up.
> * Use expression.
> * Don't talk or play while on stage.
> * Background needs to sit still and be quiet so as not to be distracting.
> * Pay attention.
> * Wait for the audience to stop clapping before speaking again.

Vocabulary Building with *Geology Rocks!*

Here are some words from the show that are worth knowing!

Geologic Terms

geology	gravel	opal
Richter scale	marble	sapphire
volcano	limestone	emerald
earthquake	granite	ruby
seismograph	fossil fuel	rock cycle
tectonic plate	natural gas	sediment
continental plate	oil	geo-thermal
basalt	coal	geologic time
fault	decompose	
San Andreas fault	miners	
igneous	precious metal	
metamorphic	sea shore	
sedimentary	valley	
Colorado river	erosion	
canyon	weathering	
desert	plateau	
ocean	Himalayas	
mountain	mineral	
molten rock/magma	silver	
pyroclastic	iron	
Mt. St. Helens	gold	
vent	diamond	
ore	copper	
mantel	aluminum	
core	nickel	
crust	lead	

Other Words and Phrases

alternative	innocent
dramatic	sledges
deduction	PR
suspicious	CPA
drastic	gig
SUV	inert
sculpt	souvenir
gouge	spunk
mutinous	elude
Yanks	voila
belch	

"Not just another pretty face"
"Why I never!"
"slow as rock"
"Rome wasn't built in a day"

Emphasis: Making the Words come Alive

One of the challenges in putting on children's plays is to get your students to treat the lyrics and dialogue as language, to speak and sing in natural rhythms. The key is to have the students emphasize the right words and syllables. Kids often sound great when they're singing but terrible during dialogue. You need to model speaking with expression. Have them analyze their lines for action words—exciting words that make the lines come alive. Then show them how to stress these words to bring out the meaning. Scenes always work best when the actors know which words need to be stressed. Again, we suggest video-taping the dialogue so students can discover what they really sound like.

Final Performance

Your most important performance will probably be for the students' parents and families. There is a tradeoff in setting the time. More people can come if you do it in the evening, but the problem is that you'll have to go back to school and all your kids will have to remember (and be able) to return. Many teachers perform only during regular school hours.

If Something Goes Wrong: Ignore it!

Tell your students that if something goes wrong, they should continue with the play as though nothing was amiss. It won't help to stop and tell fellow actors what to do.

If you're new to this you might be a bit nervous. Remember that the parents are there to watch their children and they'll be pleased with almost anything. When it comes out well, you'll be a star. If it comes out wonderfully, you'll be nominated for Teacher of the Century. As we suggested above, we strongly urge you to do a number of informal performances (dress rehearsals) for other classes. You might start with younger kids, since they tend to be easily impressed. Then move up to the students' peers and older kids. Since the shows are informal it's okay to stop the action if the kids are having some problems. The main thing is to let them get used to performing. Don't worry if your musician (if you have chosen to use one) isn't available for every performance—just use the audio recording.

During the show you should be in clear view of the students. You're there to help the kids remember what they need to do and encourage them when they do well. You can cue all group singing and mouth the lyrics to help keep the class together. If some of the lyrics seem difficult to memorize, you may want to hold up signs with key words or pictures to remind the kids what comes next. Some teachers just go ahead and sing along on the group songs.

Print up a program, and don't forget the invitations to the parents. A cast party is traditional after the last performance of a play. The kids will really enjoy it and it will provide a great chance for the parents to talk with one another and congratulate themselves for managing to arrange such a wonderful teacher for their kids. (This may sound flippant but we've heard people say things like this at every post-performance party we've attended. There's nothing like a genuinely good school play to fill parents with joy and gratitude.)

Turning on the Applause Sign

The audience wants to applaud, but it needs to be told when it's the right time to clap. Since you have no applause sign, the actions themselves of the student actors must say loudly and clearly, "Okay, we're done with the scene, you can applaud now." To convey this message to the audience, the performing students need to do two things: they must stop all movement, and they must face the audience. If they start moving the second they finish the song, the audience will not know the scene is completed. Finally, don't be afraid to clap yourself at the right moment. The students deserve it, and the audience will follow your lead. This is especially important after the very first song. If those watching the show understand at the beginning that they are allowed and expected to show their appreciation, they will continue to do so throughout the show.

Last Bit of Advice

When you're learning to cook, you follow the cookbook to the letter. If the recipe calls for 1 1/2 cups of fresh smelt, you put in 1 1/2 cups of fresh smelt. Later, after you gain some confidence, you loosen up and take some chances. The same thing  happens with putting on a play—after a few tries, you'll be spicing up the show at every turn. We've tried to give you an accurate and workable recipe for a really fun show, but feel free to do anything that seems best for you and your class. And if you have any great ideas, or even good ones, please contact us so we can include them in the next version of this show.

The Complete Piano/Guitar Music for *Geology Rocks!*

The complete score for piano and guitar accompaniment is available from Bad Wolf Press.

This compilation includes all the music for *Geology Rocks!* and is in an easy piano style with complete guitar chord suggestions. It is absolutely necessary if you plan live musical accompaniment of the show. Budding piano students may also enjoy playing some of the catchy tunes including "Geologic Time," "I Am Deep," and "Seven Little Miners."

Ordering *Geology Rocks!* for Students

Many students and their families would like to own their very own copies of this book and recording, a souvenir to remind them of the great time they had being a part of the show. We think this is highly commendable, so...

Bad Wolf Press proudly announces the **Musicals for Munchkins** program. Here's how it works. Your students can buy this book and tape for half-price as long as at least seven books are purchased at the same time. One check only is to be sent and we will ship all the books to the same address. It's the perfect and inexpensive way for a teacher to put high-quality literature, music and art into young impressionable minds.

The fine print: this offer is for student use only. No one who buys through the **Musicals for Munchkins** program is authorized to produce this show. Teachers may purchase copies at regular retail price only. We are cheerfully making this show available to students at a price barely above cost. Please don't take unauthorized advantage of our simple-mindedness and turn us into just another crestfallen and cynical team of songwriters squeezing the last nickel out of the innocent children of America.

And if you liked *Geology Rocks!*, you have to try our other equally flavorful musicalizations.

To order from Bad Wolf Press

For a complete list of musicals available from Bad Wolf Press, please contact us at any of the addresses or numbers listed below.

Would you like to be on our mailing list? You'll receive our superior-quality newsletter that includes many ideas from teachers on how they work with musicals in their own classrooms. This newsletter (*Big Bad Wolf*) comes out as often as we have the time to put it out and some folks like it so much that whenever a new issue comes they take a couple days off work just to savor it.

Have you any ideas or suggestions regarding musicals? Let us know so we can alert the rest of the civilized world.

Please contact us at: Bad Wolf Press
                          5391 Spindrift Court
                          Camarillo, CA 93012
                          Toll Free: 1-888-827-8661
                          www.badwolfpress.com